Smile

Smile

Raina Telgemeier

with color by Stephanie Yue

graphix

An Imprint of

SCHOLASTIC

New York Toronto London Auckland Sydney Mexico City New Delhi Hong Kong

This graphic novel is based on personal experiences, though some names have been changed, and certain characters, places, and incidents have been modified in service of the story.

Library of Congress Cataloging-in-Publication Data
Telgemeier, Raina.
Smile / Raina Telgemeier. – 1st ed.
p. cm.
ISBN: 978-0-545-13205-3 (hardcover)
ISBN: 978-0-545-13206-0 (paperback)
1. Youth–Dental care. 2. Girls–Dental care. 3. Self-esteem in adolescence.
4. Beauty, Personal. 5. Graphic novels. I. Title.
RK55.Y68.T45 2010
617.6'45–dc22
2008051782

50 49 48 47 46 45 44 43 19 20

First edition, February 2010
Edited by Cassandra Pelham
Book design by Phil Falco and John Green
Creative Director: David Saylor
Printed in Malaysia 108

For Dave

Dentistry &
Orthodontics
PARKING

CHAPTER ONE

SMILE!!

FLASH!

GOOD! LET'S GET YOU SET UP IN A CHAIR, AND THE ORTHODONTIST WILL LOOK AT YOUR TEETH IN A FEW MINUTES.
SANI-GLOVES

HI, RAINA! I'M DR. DRAGONI.
HI...

SO, YOU'RE IN SIXTH GRADE? WHERE DO YOU GO TO SCHOOL?
HJKMP TSS...

I STILL DON'T SEE WHY I NEED BRACES, MOM. MY TEETH LOOK OKAY TO **ME**.
C'MON, WILL.

YOU HAVE AN OVERBITE, HONEY. IT'S SOMETHING THAT CAN CAUSE PROBLEMS LATER IF YOU DON'T GET IT FIXED.
OH.

YOU'RE GONNA BE A **METAL-MOUTH!!**
AMARA, PLEASE DON'T TEASE HER...

HAVE A GOOD TIME AT YOUR SCOUT MEETING, OKAY? KELLI'S MOM WILL DRIVE YOU HOME LATER.
'KAY. THANKS, MOM.

YOU'RE GETTING BRACES, TOO? IT'S NOT THAT BAD.
Jill, Troop Leader
Kaylah
Emily
Kelli
Jenny
Raina (me)
Melissa
Karin
Nicole
LUCK

YOU CAN'T CHEW POPCORN... OR APPLES... OR CARROTS. OR GUM. OR TAFFY. OR CARAMEL. OR...

MAYBE THAT MEANS I'LL STOP CHEWING MY NAILS, TOO!!

An hour later
...AND AT OUR NEXT MEETING, WE'LL BE MAKING EASTER BASKETS! SEE YOU THEN!
BYE!

IS IT OKAY IF I DROP YOU OFF FIRST, RAINA?
SURE.

KELLI, YOU AND MELISSA WALK RAINA TO HER PORCH, OKAY?
RACE YOU GUYS!!

LAST ONE TO THE PORCH IS A ROTTEN EGG!!

...WAIT UP!!

KELLI--

GRAB!

STUMBLE

TRIP

WHAM!

...RAINA?

...

HANDS... LEGS...

NOTHING BROKEN.
COOL.

?

RAINA?
OW...

ARE YOU OKAY?

AAAAAAA!!!
OH MY GOSH!

WHAT HAPPENED?
GO GET HER MOM! QUICK!!

IT'S OKAY, HONEY... IT'S GONNA BE OKAY.
MY TEETH!!!

...HUH?

AH!
GRAB

MY TOOTH!!

HONEY?! OH MY GOODNESS...

WE'VE GOT ONE TOOTH... ANYBODY FIND THE OTHER?
I DON'T SEE IT.
NOPE, NOTHING HERE...

DADDY? WHAT'S GOING ON?
YOUR SISTER'S HAD AN ACCIDENT. TRY AND GO BACK TO SLEEP, OKAY?

D
Denis office
(408) 555-6372
Dentist
(415) 555-1291
After-hours
(415) 555-3741
E
Emily (415) 555-2650
Ethel
(415) 555-0706

MILK... YOU PUT A TOOTH IN MILK...

SURE...TWENTY MINUTES?
2%
Berke
Farm

WE'LL BE RIGHT THERE.

...BYE.

HEY, MOM!
I LOOK LIKE I'M SIX AGAIN!!

HA HA HA HA HA!
SHE'S IN SHOCK.

WE'RE LUCKY DR. GOLDEN IS STILL AT HIS OFFICE THIS LATE!!

SO YOU COULDN'T FIND THE SECOND TOOTH?
NOPE.

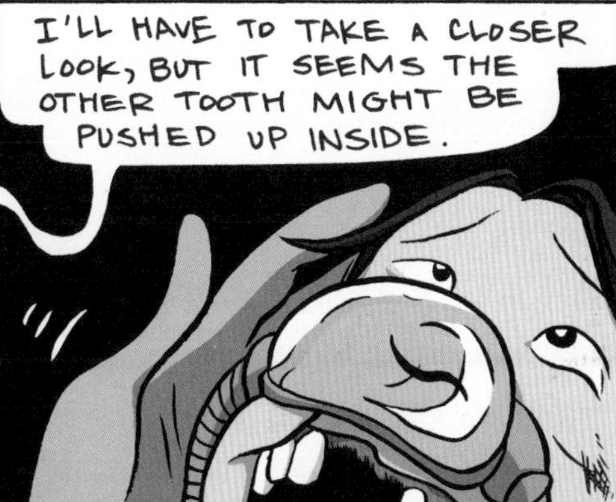
I'LL HAVE TO TAKE A CLOSER LOOK, BUT IT SEEMS THE OTHER TOOTH MIGHT BE PUSHED UP INSIDE.

YOU OKAY, RAINA?
UH-HUH...

I don't remember the rest of that night too well.

Dr. Golden put the tooth that fell out back in place...

...and pulled the other one down from out of my gum (where it was stuck).

Novocaine, nitrous, and codeine in my sleepy, overwhelmed body...

...made the whole thing seem like a weird dream.

Tweet
Tweet

Blink
Blink

MOM??

OH, HONEY, YOU'RE AWAKE! HOW ARE YOU FEELING? DO YOU WANT SOMETHING TO DRINK?

WHAT'TH THITH THTUFF ON MY TEETH??

DR. GOLDEN SAID IT'S SORT OF LIKE A CAST. IT'LL KEEP YOUR TEETH IN PLACE WHILE THEY HEAL.
OH.

SIP
I DON'T FEEL GOOD.

I KNOW, BUT YOU GET TO STAY HOME FROM SCHOOL.
TRUE!!

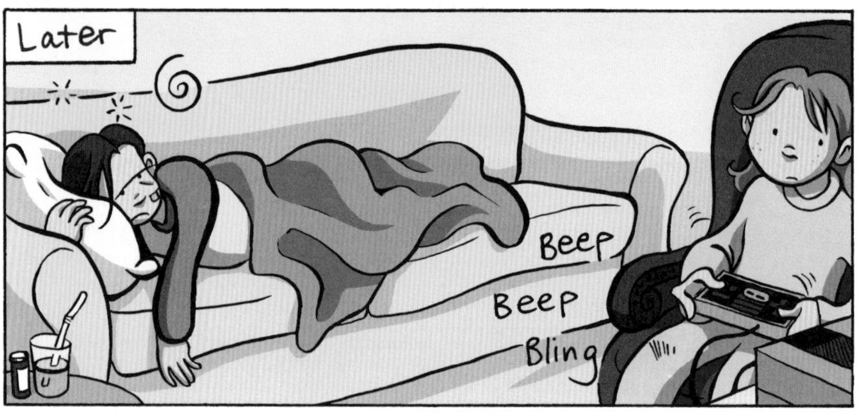
Later
Beep
Beep
Bling

BLOOP!
AW!

YOU CAN ONLY WATCH YOUR SISTER DIE AT SUPER MARIO BROTHERS SO MANY TIMES...
Beep
Boop
Beep

...RAINA?

I DROPPED BY YOUR SCHOOL TO PICK UP YOUR HOME-WORK.

MR. CRUZ SENT THIS ALONG, TOO.
THANKTH, DAD...

RRRIP

SMILE
wishes
eel better, Tony

...YEAH, RIGHT.
SMILE

The following week

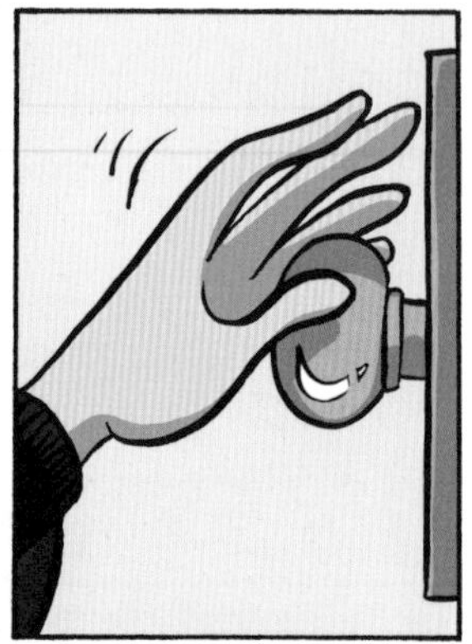

DIDJA HEAR SHE KNOCKED ALL HER TEETH OUT?
HOW?

...FIGHT...
... GYM CLASS...
...DOWN A STAIR-WAY...

SO, RAINA, WHY DON'T YOU TELL THE CLASS WHAT HAPPENED? WE'VE ALL BEEN SO CURIOUS.
Language Arts

UH...

I... I WATH RUNNING, AND I FELL. MY TWO FRONT TEETH CAME OUT.

LEMME SEE?!
UM...

WHAT'S THAT WHITISH STUFF IN THERE?
OKAY, JUAN, LET'S LEAVE HER ALONE FOR NOW...

SO HOW DID IT HAPPEN?
DID IT HURT?
WHAT KIND OF MEDICINE DID YOU GET?
HOW DO YOU EAT?
DID YOU CRY?

UM... WELL...

HEY, GUYS... HEY, RAINA.

HOWYA FEELIN'?
HI, KELLI.

MOM, I'M THICK OF TAKING THEETH PILLTH.
I KNOW, KIDDO.

BUT YOU HAVE TO FINISH THE PRESCRIPTION.
GLUNK

BLEH... I FEEL LIKE THROWING UP.

YOU'VE EATEN NOTHING BUT ICE CREAM, CHICKEN BROTH, AND CODEINE FOR A WEEK...

...OF COURSE YOU FEEL NAUSEOUS.

ARE YOU READY TO GO, HONEY?
YEAH.

THO, WHAT'TH DR. GOLDEN GONNA DO?
TAKE OFF THE "CAST"... DO SOME X-RAYS... SEE IF YOUR TEETH ARE HEALING.

OKAY.

I WONDER IF MY ACCTHIDENT WATH THE WORTHT THING HE EVER THAW?

HONEY, LOTS OF KIDS HAVE ACCIDENTS. HE'S SEEN KNOCKED-OUT TEETH BEFORE.

MY STAR PATIENT!!
PUSH

GLAD TO SEE YOU FEELING BETTER, RAINA! YOU TOOK QUITE A FALL THAT NIGHT!
OPEN.

SO WE'RE JUST GOING TO REMOVE THE PLASTER SEAL...

YOU'LL BE ABLE TO SEE YOUR TEETH AGAIN!
TUG

pop

UH-OH.

HM...
WHAT?!

WHEN YOU KNOCKED THEM OUT, YOU MUST HAVE DAMAGED THE BONE ABOVE, TOO...
CAN I SEE?
SO WHEN I PUT THEM BACK IN PLACE, THEY WENT UP FARTHER...
I'M SURE THERE'S SOME WAY WE CAN FIX THIS...
I LOOK LIKE A VAMPIRE!!

LET'S LOOK AT YOUR X-RAYS...

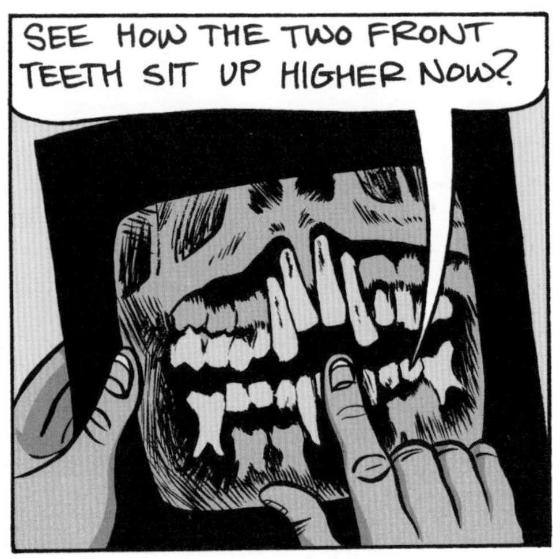
SEE HOW THE TWO FRONT TEETH SIT UP HIGHER NOW?

CAN YOU BRING HER FAMILY BACK HERE?
SURE.

...LOOKS LIKE THERE'S SOME NERVE DAMAGE TO THE FRONT FOUR...
LEMME SEE?

...TO AN ENDODONTIST FOR ROOT CANALS...
C'MON, SIS!
OKAY...

...TRY TO SAVE THOSE TEETH, SO SHE'S NOT WEARING DENTURES AT ELEVEN YEARS OLD...
HA HA HA!

HA HA! YOU LOOK LIKE A LITTLE KID AGAIN!

AN' I ONLY JUST GOT MY PERMANENT FRONT TEETH ABOUT A YEAR AGO.
BUT YOU JUST LOST YOU
AMARA!!

STOP.

COME ON, GIRLS. WE'RE GOING TO TOYS "R" US.

RAINA GETS TO CHOOSE A GET-WELL PRESENT.
HEY!

Soon
AW, C'MON... YOU DON'T REALLY WANNA GET STUPID WIZARDS & WARRIORS, DO YA? HOW 'BOUT DUCKTALES?
WHAT IF WE GOT CALIFORNIA GAMES? HUH?

Beep
WIZARDS & WARRIORS

COOL! CHECK IT OUT... THE BOOTS OF LAVA WALK!

CAN I PLAY?
NO.

MOM, WHY IS RAINA ACTING LIKE SUCH A JERK LATELY?

SHE'S IN PAIN, AMARA. IF PLAYING NINTENDO NONSTOP MAKES HER FORGET ABOUT HER TEETH...
...I KINDA THINK WE SHOULD LET HER PLAY.

SHE HAS A LOT MORE PAIN TO LOOK FORWARD TO... SO TRY AND GO EASY ON HER, OKAY?
HMPH.
AND "JERK" ISN'T A VERY NICE WORD.

CHAPTER TWO

WHATCHA THINKIN', RAINA?
I'M NERVOUS ABOUT GIRL SCOUTS. LAST TIME WE MET WAS WHEN I HAD MY ACCIDENT.

THINGS'LL BE FINE. YOU'LL SEE.

SO WE WANNA SEE!!

UM...YOU DON'T LOOK THAT WEIRD.
YEAH.
UH, YEAH. JUST A LITTLE FUNNY.
IT'S...NOT AS BAD AS...BEFORE.
WOW.

ARE THEY GONNA GET FIXED?
WELL, I'M S'POSED TO GET BRACES ANYWAY, SO THEY'RE GONNA TRY TO PULL THESE TWO DOWN.

SO, IT'S TEMPORARY? DON'T WORRY ABOUT IT, THEN!

I WAS AFRAID IT MADE ME LOOK LIKE A SIX-YEAR-OLD!

NO... BUT YOU KNOW WHAT DOES MAKE YOU LOOK LIKE A BABY?
WHAT?

THOSE PONYTAILS!

THANKS FOR DRIVING ME HOME AGAIN.
OF COURSE.

...AND RAINA? BE CAREFUL!

...LET'S WALK TO YOUR HOUSE THIS TIME.
GOOD IDEA.

I DO LOOK LIKE A BABY.
TUG

BUT DO I REALLY CARE WHAT ANY-ONE ELSE THINKS?

...YES.

MR. CRUZ? I WON'T BE IN CLASS TOMORROW... HERE'S MY DENTIST'S NOTE.

OKAY...LET ME GIVE YOU THE CHAPTERS WE'LL BE READING FOR HOMEWORK...
MISSING SCHOOL? LUCKY!!
FLIP FLIP

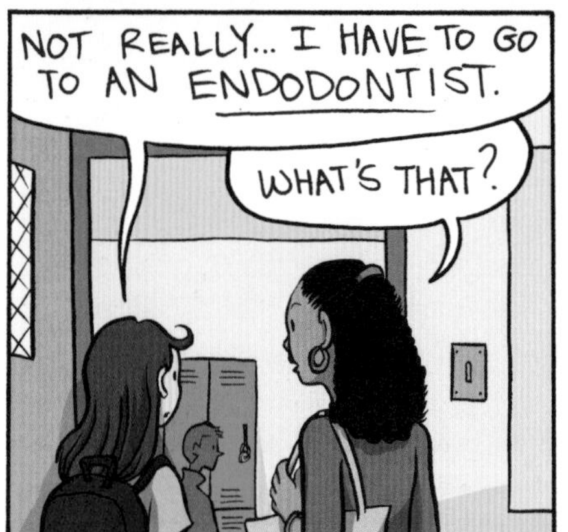
NOT REALLY... I HAVE TO GO TO AN ENDODONTIST.
WHAT'S THAT?

...I'M NOT EXACTLY SURE!
TIGERS

WELL, THE NAME MAKES IT SOUND LIKE IT'LL BE THE END OF YOU!!
106.1 KMEL
NKOTB

BLAH BLAH BLAH, ROOT CANALS BLAH...

BLAHSE-BLAH... HOLES DRILLED IN YOUR TEETH, BLAH-DE-BLAH...

DUM DUM, THREE HOURS OR LONGER DOO DOO DUM...

DOOT DOOT NOVOCAINE... DOOBEE DOO...

YADA YADA LAUGHING GAS, BLOO-BLAH...

BLAH...

HERE, YOU CAN LISTEN TO THE RADIO WHILE WE WORK.
?

After that it was sort of peaceful.

I got up once during the surgery to use the bathroom.

There were clamps, a plastic guard, and gauze in and around my mouth.

It looked cool!
HA HA!

They had to give me several novocaine shots because they kept wearing off and things would start to hurt.
THERE WE GO.

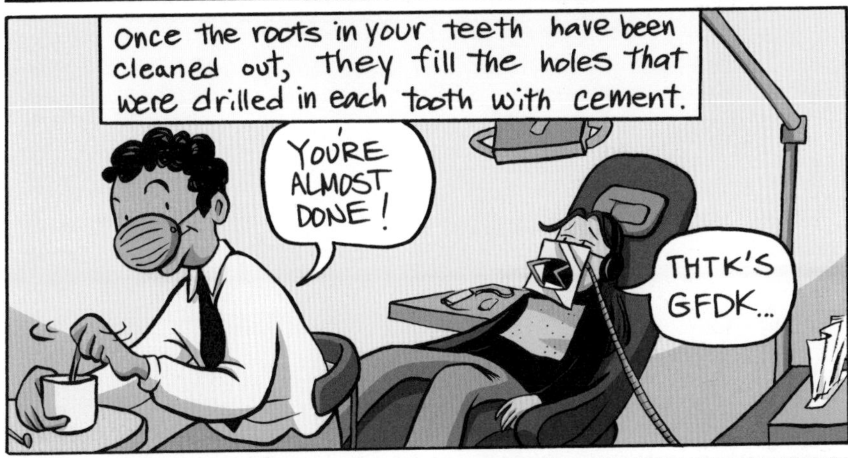
Once the roots in your teeth have been cleaned out, they fill the holes that were drilled in each tooth with cement.
YOU'RE ALMOST DONE!
THTK'S GFDK...

The cement is sealed with a red-hot metal tool...

...which I SMELLED as it accidentally touched the roof of my mouth before I felt it.
HISSSSS
OOOOO! SORRY!

A few weeks later

WELL, KIDDO... YOU'RE ALMOST TWELVE!
YEAH...

IS THERE ANYTHING SPECIAL YOU'D LIKE TO DO FOR YOUR BIRTHDAY?

...

CAN I GET MY EARS PIERCED?

WHY WOULD YOU WANT TO DO THAT? YOU'VE NEVER BEEN INTERESTED IN PIERCING THEM BEFORE!

WHAT IF WE WAIT TILL AFTER YOUR BIRTHDAY TO GET THEM PIERCED?
PIZZA PIZZ

YOU ARE GETTING YOUR BRACES PRETTY SOON...

MAYBE THAT COULD BE YOUR REWARD, AND YOUR BIRTHDAY PRESENT.
OKAY!
OPEN

KAYLAH TOLD ME ABOUT A GOOD JEWELRY PLACE WHERE SHE GOT HERS DONE.
ZZA PIZZ

...AN' I SAW THESE FRESH EARRINGS AT CONTEMPO THE OTHER DAY...MELISSA HAS A PAIR OF LIGHT-NING BOLTS...I WANNA GET SOME LIKE BRANDY ON THE NEW MICKEY MOUSE CLUB HAS, TOO...

A few days later

SMILE?

HMM.

I GUESS WE'LL HAVE TO TAKE A NEW POLAROID.
BRACES ARE ACES!

YOUR MOUTH LOOKS PRETTY DIFFERENT FROM THE LAST TIME YOU WERE HERE!

WE'LL START WITH THE BRACKETS ON THE TWO FRONTS...

...AND BAND HER MOLARS.
TELGEMEIER, RAINA

THAT WAY, SHE CAN START WITH THE HEADGEAR RIGHT AWAY.
HEAD-GEAR?!

SURE. FIXING YOUR OVER-BITE WAS THE WHOLE POINT TO BEGIN WITH.

BUT... BUT I'M GONNA LOOK LIKE A NERD WITH HEADGEAR ON!

YOU ONLY NEED TO WEAR IT AT NIGHT!

JAMIE, ARE YOU READY WITH THAT?

WE'RE MAKING A MOLD OF YOUR MOUTH. OPEN UP... THIS MIGHT FEEL A LITTLE UNCOMFORTABLE...

SHOVE!

THE IMPRESSION MATERIAL HAS TO HARDEN, SO JUST KEEP YOUR MOUTH CLOSED AND TRY TO RELAX.

TICK
TICK

TICK
TICK

ALL RIGHT. YOU'RE DONE.
PTAH!

TEN MORE SECONDS AND I WOULD HAVE PUKED!

NOW FOR THE BOTTOM TEETH!
AAA!!

TIME TO OPEN YOUR PRESENTS!

EARRINGS!

...EARRINGS!
OOO, CUTE!

...EARRINGS!

NOW YOU **HAVE** TO LET ME PIERCE MY EARS, MOM!
I KNOW, I KNOW...

WHEN DO YOU GET YOUR BRACES, RAINA?

FRIDAY.

WHAT ABOUT YOUR EARS, WHEN DO YOU GET THEM PIERCED?

'BOUT A WEEK LATER.

COOL, SO YOU'LL LOOK NORMAL SOON?
joy of ooking

Back at the orthodontist...
TWIST
TWIST
TWIST
SCRAPE
TIGHTEN
TWIST
PUSH
YANK
SHOVE
PULL
TWIST
TWIST

THAT'S IT!

Braces work through subtle pressure.

Little by little, the pressure is increased.
KINDA WEIRD, HUH?
YEAH!

And little by little, teeth move.
MY LIPS AREN'T USED TO THEM YET.

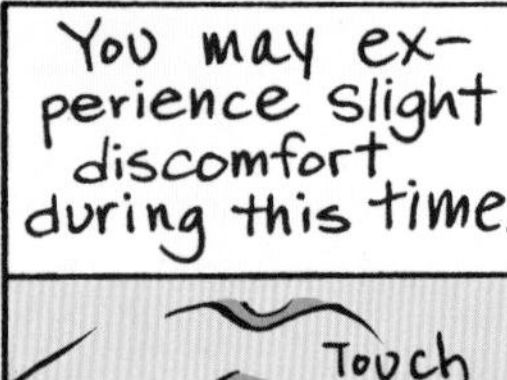
You may experience slight discomfort during this time.

Touch

OWW!!

OW!
222

OW!

OW!
Mashed Potatoes

OW!

OW!

MY **WHOLE HEAD** HURTS **SO MUCH**!

WHY DON'T YOU BANG IT AGAINST THE WALL A FEW TIMES?

THAT WAY, WHEN YOU STOP BANGING...
?

...IT'LL HURT LESS!!
THANKS FOR THE SYMPA-THY, DAD.

AW, C'MON ... LET'S GO SEE A MOVIE OR SOMETHING. WANT TO COME, WILL?
YEAH!

CAN WE GET POP-CORN, DADDY?
HMM ...

RAINA'S NOT SUPPOSED TO EAT POP-CORN WHILE SHE HAS HER BRACES...
EH, IT'S OKAY... WILL CAN STILL HAVE SOME.
I'M NOT THAT INTO POPCORN ANYWAY.
GIANTS

POP POP POP POP POP POP
POPCORN
SNIFF
SNIFF

OF COURSE, AS SOON AS YOU CAN'T HAVE SOMETHING, IT STARTS TO SMELL AMAZING!!
POP POP POP POP
POP POP
POPCORN POPCORN

OW...
Oatmeal

RAINA... ARE YOU SURE YOU WANT TO GET YOUR EARS PIERCED TODAY?
SURE I'M SURE!

OKAY... I JUST WONDERED, BECAUSE YOUR TEETH ARE HURTING YOU SO MUCH THAT...
MOM!

IT'S DIFFERENT. I DIDN'T REALLY WANT BRACES... BUT I **WANT** EARRINGS.
OKAY.

SO WHAT IF I'M AFRAID OF NEEDLES?
I WANT TO DO THIS!

...I THINK...

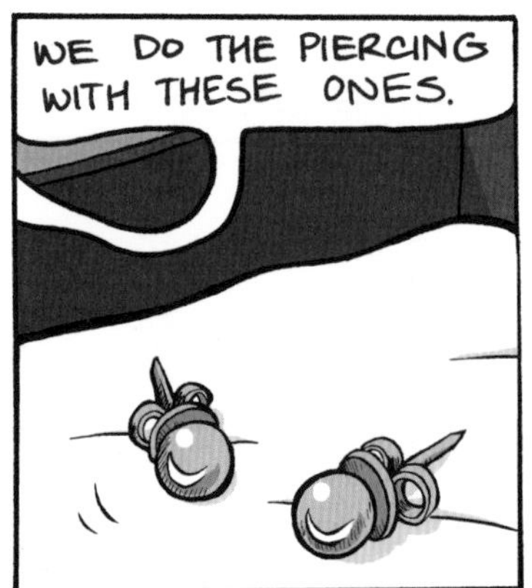
WE DO THE PIERCING WITH THESE ONES.

OKAY...

WE DRAW A DOT WHERE THE EAR-RING GOES...

NOW WE PIERCE. TAKE A DEEP BREATH.
SSNNNNNNNFFFR

CHAGUNK!

CHAGUNK!

DONE!

SEE? VERY PRETTY!

THAT DIDN'T EVEN HURT MUCH, MOM!
THAT'S GOOD!

SALINE TO KEEP THEM MOIST... ANTIBACTERIAL OINTMENT SO IT DOESN'T GET INFECTED...

I'M STARTING TO FEEL LIKE A REAL TEENAGER!
SIGH!

The next day
dab dab
OW...
RING

HEY, JANE! YEAH. OH, MAYBE... LET ME SEE IF MY MOM CAN DRIVE ME OVER TO YOUR HOUSE.

Soon
DO YOU WISH JANE HADN'T MOVED TO A DIFFERENT TOWN, RAINA?
YEAH, SOMETIMES.

SHE WAS MY BEST FRIEND UNTIL FIFTH GRADE.
I MISS HAVING HER AROUND.

SHE'S THE ONLY FRIEND I HAVE WHO'S LESS MATURE THAN ME!
PRECIOUS
KITTY

SO... WHAT DO YOU THINK?
YOU LOOK ABOUT THE SAME.

AW, C'MON, JANE. DO I LOOK COOLER? OLDER?
I GUESS.

HEY, IS YOUR DAD HERE? MAYBE HE COULD DRIVE US TO THE MALL!
HE'S AT WORK.

DARN. I WANTED TO FIND SOME BOYS TO HANG OUT WITH.

MARIO

...I GUESS I JUST WISH BOYS LIKED ME.

SO NONE OF THEM DO? ARE YOU SURE?

HOW COULD THEY, WITH MY FACE ALL MESSED UP LIKE THIS?
OH, WHAT-EVER.

THERE'S GOTTA BE SOME-ONE AT YOUR SCHOOL WHO LIKES YOU.

WELL...JEREMIAH LIKES ME...AND ABRAHAM...AND ELIAS...SO DO DAN, AND ANDRE, AND MATT P... OH, AND AARON, AND STEPHEN...

BUT THEY DON'T COUNT, I MEAN CUTE BOYS!

CHAPTER THREE

That summer was pretty normal, as summers go.

Girl Scout Camp

Grandma

Nintendo

Fog

Car trips

Orthodontist

Oh, and also...
HEADGEAR.

CLIP

C'MON, MOM, LET'S GO GET ME SOME GLASSES, A POCKET PROTECTOR, AND SOME VELCRO SHOES.

HONEY, IT'S NOT THAT BAD.

AND YOU ONLY NEED TO WEAR IT WHILE YOU SLEEP!
OW.

LOTS OF KIDS WEAR FUNNY STUFF TO HELP FIX THEIR BODIES...

...YOU PROBABLY JUST DON'T REALIZE IT BE-CAUSE NO ONE TALKS ABOUT IT.
SHOPPING LIST

WELL, MAYBE SOMEONE SHOULD START TALKING ABOUT IT !!

MAYBE IT WOULD MAKE US FEEL LESS LIKE FREAKS.

I GUESS IN SOME WAYS, I AM KINDA NORMAL...

LOTS OF KIDS WEAR BRACES, AFTER ALL.

LOTS OF KIDS HAVE...

WHAT THE...?

GREAT. THE FIRST DAY OF SEVENTH GRADE AND I'M TOTALLY BREAKING OUT.
GUESS ?

MELISSA... I'VE TURNED INTO A BRACE-FACE AND A ZIT-FACE!! WHAT AM I SUPPOSED TO DO?!
I DUNNO.

EVERYONE'S GONNA NOTICE!

LOOKIT ALL THESE LITTLE KIDS! AAAA! TINY-TOT SIXTH GRADERS EVERYWHERE!!
GUESS ?

UNLESS EVERYONE AROUND ME IS TOO SCARED TO NOTICE!!
GIANTS

WHAT'S YOUR CLASS SCHEDULE LIKE?
NOT BAD...
FIRST PERIOD ART, SECOND PERIOD PRE-ALGEBRA, THIRD PERIOD LANGUAGE ARTS, FOURTH PERIOD SOCIAL STUDIES, FIFTH PERIOD LUNCH, SIXTH PERIOD GYM, SEVENTH PERIOD BEGINNING BAND.

EW, YOU HAVE GYM RIGHT BEFORE BAND CLASS?
SO?

SO YOU'LL SMELL FUNNY DURING SEVENTH PERIOD.

EMILY, BEGINNING BAND'S GONNA BE ME AN' A BUNCH OF SIXTH GRADERS. I DON'T CARE WHAT THEY THINK OF ME.

OKAY! WELCOME, CLASS. I'M MR. DOUGLAS. IS EVERYONE SITTING IN THE RIGHT SECTIONS? FLUTES IN FRONT, CLARINETS OVER HERE, SAXES ON THIS SIDE...

OH, MAN, THIS GUY WON'T STOP LOOKIN' AT ME...
HE'S PRETTY CUTE!

ACK, BUT IF I SMILE BACK, HE'LL SEE THAT MY TEETH ARE...

CHRISTINE?
HERE.
JORDAN?
HERE.
SAMUEL?
HERE... YOU CAN CALL ME SAMMY.
B.V.M

RAINA?
HERE.

FIRST THINGS FIRST. IT'S TIME TO LEARN TO ASSEMBLE YOUR INSTRUMENTS.
SO, UH... YOU'RE IN SIXTH, RIGHT?

YEAH-- WHY, WHAT GRADE ARE YOU IN?
SEVENTH.

REALLY?! SEVENTH?!
WOW! OH MY GOSH. WOW.

THAT'S ENOUGH FOR TODAY, CLASS. PRACTICE THOSE FIVE NOTES TONIGHT FOR HOMEWORK!

SO, UM... BYE.

BYE.

JEEZ, WHAT HAPPENED TO YOU?!
WHAT? C'MON, TELL ME!
HEY, RAINA!
GUESS
?

That evening

!!

PANT
PANT

NOW MY HANDS HURT AS MUCH AS MY TEETH!

San Francisco summers are cold and foggy... but October is usually a sunny month.

And like every year, this brought a feeling of optimism into the air.

Like something good was about to happen.

MAYBE I'LL DO MY HOMEWORK EARLY.

ALPHONSO, FROM NOW ON...

HEY, MOM, WHAT ARE WE --

HEAVE!

EARTHQUAKE.
EARTHQUAKE.

WILL!!
DROP
RATTLE BOOM SHAKE

WILL!! DON'T JUST STAND THERE!! COME HERE QUICK!!!
TIDE
OH MY GOSH.
OH MY GOSH.
HUH?
XEROX
That was the first time my sister voluntarily hugged me... and the only time I've ever heard her pray.
And just as soon as it had started...
Mumble Mumble
BOOOMMMMMHHHHMMMMMoooo

... it was over.

WILL!!!
WHAT?
RALLY

THANK GOODNESS THESE BOOK-SHELVES ARE BOLTED TO THE WALL... THEY COULD'VE FALLEN ON YOU, WILL.
OH.
OH MY GOSH!!

DID YOU SEE THE FLOOR?! IT WAS BOUNCING UP AND DOWN!
IT WENT UP, LIKE, A FOOT!

MOM! SOME OF DAD'S FILE CABINETS FELL!
WHOA!

I DON'T THINK ANYTHING'S BROKEN, THOUGH.
YOUR DAD'S STILL AT WORK. I HOPE HE'S ALL RIGHT.
WE SHOULD TURN ON THE NEWS!

CLICK

THE POWER'S OUT.
OH, RIGHT.

EVERYONE IS OUT ON THEIR PORCHES!
...7.5 ON THE RICHTER SCALE...
I HEARD IT WAS 8.2!

YOU FOLKS OKAY? YOUR HUSBAND OKAY?
YES, HE JUST CALLED... HE'S ON HIS WAY HOME.

DID YOU HEAR? THE WHOLE BAY BRIDGE COLLAPSED!!
222

MOM FINALLY FOUND SOME "D" BATTERIES.

... PARTIAL COLLAPSE OF THE NIMITZ FREEWAY AND THE WEST-BOUND SECTION OF THE BAY BRIDGE... FIRES BURNING IN THE MARINA, THOUSANDS FEARED DEAD OR INJURED...

RATTLE RATTLE
RATTLE
RATTLE

AFTER-SHOCK.

I SUPPOSE WE'D BETTER GET OUT THE SLEEPING BAGS... WE'D BE BETTER OFF SLEEPING DOWN HERE IN THE LIVING ROOM, JUST IN CASE.
LIKE CAMPING!

Two hours later
I'M HOME!
DAD!

I'M SO GLAD YOU'RE ALL SAFE! IT'S A NIGHTMARE OUT THERE. THE ROADS ARE JAMMED, EVERYONE'S IN A PANIC, IT'S ABSOLUTE CHAOS. DID YOU SEE THE APARTMENT TOWERS OVER BY 19th AVENUE? THEY'RE CRACKED AND CRUMBLING!

MY BUDDY FRANK LIVES IN WATSONVILLE, I HEARD THAT'S WHERE THE QUAKE'S EPICENTER WAS...
HE HASN'T BEEN ABLE TO GET IN CONTACT WITH HIS FAMILY YET.

THE PHONE LINES ARE SO OVERBURDENED, IT'S ALMOST IMPOSSIBLE TO GET THROUGH TO ANYONE!
AND WORST OF ALL...

THEY HAD TO POSTPONE THE WORLD SERIES!!

IT'S SO STRANGE TO LOOK OUT OVER THE CITY WHEN ALL THE LIGHTS ARE OUT.

AND IT'S SUCH A NICE NIGHT, TOO: CLEAR, WARM, NO WIND, QUIET.

I MIGHT REALLY ENJOY THIS IF IT WEREN'T FOR THE WHOLE "GIGANTIC NATURAL CATASTROPHE" THING...

THIS IS WEIRD. IT'S ONLY 8:30... THAT'S WAY TOO EARLY TO GO TO SLEEP.

YES, BUT IT'S TOO DARK TO DO MUCH OF ANYTHING ELSE, AND WE WANT TO SAVE THE FLASHLIGHT BATTERIES IN CASE WE **REALLY** NEED THEM.

Beeeeeeeeep!!

THE MICRO-WAVE!!!
THE POWER'S BACK ON!!!
00:00

We were lucky. Our power was only out for about 3 ½ hours.
Flick!
LIIIIIIIGHT!!
YEAH!

T-VEEEEEEE!
Click

WHOA.
Earlier
FOX
I THOUGHT THE WHOLE BRIDGE FELL DOWN... THAT'S NOTHIN'.

6:15 AM
RING!

HELLO? YES? OH, HI, AUNT MARY. YES, GOOD MORNING... WE'RE ALL FINE.
Rub Rub

We got the day off from school.
THOUSANDS DEAD IN HUGE

But it wasn't very fun.
Live

And later that day, it rained. Hard. Earthquake Weather was over.
I'M GLAD WE STILL HAVE A HOME TO STAY DRY IN!

The day after that? It was BACK TO SCHOOL.
x + 3 = 7
y + 6 = 11
x + y = ?
Doodle
Doodle

Nobody could really concentrate on class work, though... not even most of the teachers.
YOU GUYS CAN HAVE A FREE PERIOD... JUST TAKE IT EASY TODAY, OKAY?

I'M GLAD YOU'RE OKAY!
ME TOO! I MEAN, JUST IMAGINE...

WHAT IF WE'D HAD AN EARTH-QUAKE WHILE SCHOOL WAS IN SESSION?!
CRUMBLE!
Oooo

ARE YOU... DOING ANYTHING AFTER SCHOOL TODAY?

MY MOM'S PICKING ME UP... I HAVE AN ORTHODONTIST'S APPOINTMENT.
WHY?
OH, UM... NO REASON.

WAS HE TRYING TO ASK ME OUT?!

HE WAS TOTALLY TRYING TO ASK ME OUT.
PARKING

GOOD THING DR. DRAGONI'S OFFICE DIDN'T FALL DOWN IN THE EARTHQUAKE, HUH?

YEAH, GOOD THING...
Prod
Push

IT'S BEEN A PRETTY STRANGE YEAR FOR YOU, HASN'T IT.
YEAH.

YOU KNOCKED OUT YOUR TWO FRONT TEETH, YOU GOT BRACES, YOU GOT YOUR EARS PIERCED...

I SURVIVED A MAJOR EARTHQUAKE...

I GUESS IN THE GRAND SCHEME OF THINGS...

LOSING A COUPLE OF TEETH ISN'T THE END OF THE WORLD!

...SIGH.

CHAPTER FOUR

RAINA LIKES A TINY-TOT SIXTH GRADER.
MELISSA!
RAINA LIKES A TINY-TOT SIXTH GRADER?

RAINA LIKES A TINY-TOT SIXTH GRADER!!
KARIN!
STOP IT!

RAINA LIKES A TINY- MMMMMPHH!!

... A TINY-TOT SIXTH GRADER LIKES ME!!

A few days before Thanksgiving
SO, THE BAD NEWS IS, YOUR TEETH AREN'T REALLY RESPONDING TO THE TREATMENT.

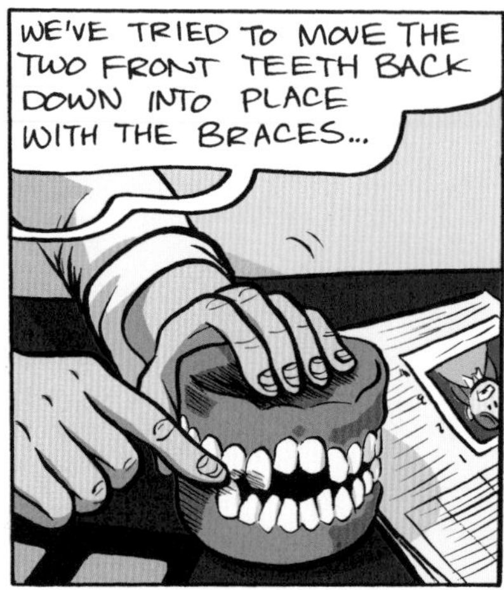
WE'VE TRIED TO MOVE THE TWO FRONT TEETH BACK DOWN INTO PLACE WITH THE BRACES...

...BUT AFTER SEVERAL MONTHS, IT JUST DOESN'T SEEM TO BE WORKING.

SO AM I GONNA LOOK LIKE A VAMPIRE FOREVER??

NO... AND THAT'S THE GOOD NEWS. I THINK WE SHOULD GIVE YOU A TEMPORARY SET OF FAKE TEETH!
IT WOULD FIRST REQUIRE A SIMPLE EXTRACTION.

"EXTRACTION"... AS IN, PULLING SOMETHING OUT?

SO, WE PULL THEM BACK OUT, AND BUILD YOU A RETAINER WITH TWO PERFECT TEETH ATTACHED TO IT, TO FILL THE GAP!

It's humiliating to let a doctor see you cry... but sometimes, it can't be helped.

RAINA, WE WANT YOU TO HAVE A FULL MOUTH OF HEALTHY TEETH.
THIS IS WHAT I PROPOSE.

THE REST OF YOUR TEETH ARE STILL FINE.

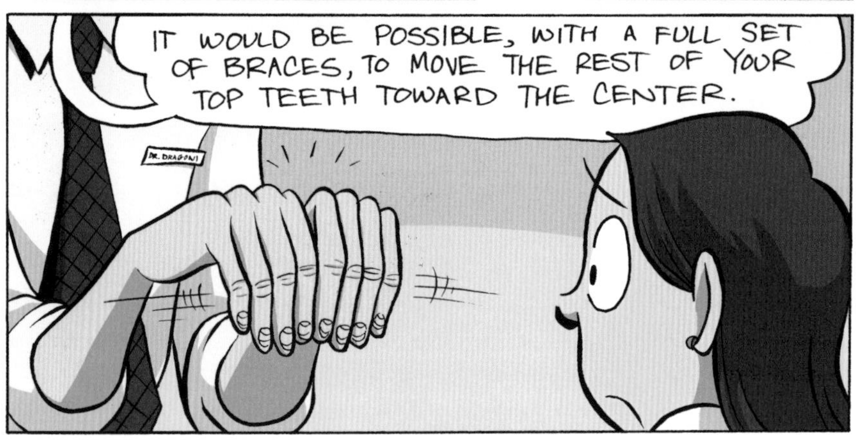
IT WOULD BE POSSIBLE, WITH A FULL SET OF BRACES, TO MOVE THE REST OF YOUR TOP TEETH TOWARD THE CENTER.
DR. DRAGONI

IT WOULD TAKE A COUPLE OF YEARS, AND IT WOULDN'T BE COSMETICALLY PERFECT, BUT IT WOULD BE VERY CLOSE.
WHAT DO YOU THINK ABOUT THAT?

WAAAAAAAAAHH!!
I GUESS WE CAN TALK IT OVER LATER.

It made sense to wait until Winter Break to pull out my teeth... then, at least, I wouldn't miss any school.
X + X =
SOMEONE IS NOT... PAYING... ATTENTION.
X = 3
Y =

Still, that meant I had weeks and weeks to worry about it.

D+

WHAT THE HECK WILL EATING BE LIKE AFTER THEY TAKE MY TEETH OUT?!

I even worried during art class, which was usually my escape from reality.
RIIIIIIIIP
EVLON

HEY, MY DAD TOOK ME TO SEE "THE LITTLE MERMAID" LAST NIGHT. IT WAS REALLY GOOD.
OH, YEAH?

YEAH. YOU SHOULD DEFINITELY GO SEE IT.

...MAYBE I WILL.

I'M TAKING YOUR SISTER AND HER FRIEND TO SEE "THE LITTLE MERMAID" TO-MORROW, RAINA... WANT TO COME WITH US?

I GUESS.
BUT **ONLY** 'CAUSE EMILY TOLD ME IT WAS GOOD.

WHATEVER. I'M TOO OLD FOR THIS DISNEY STUFF.

I'M TOTALLY GONNA HATE THIS MOVIE. I JUST KNOW IT.
WALT DISNI
PICTURES

I'M TOTALLY GONNA...
♫ I'll tell you a tale of the bottomless blue... ♫

EXIT

The Little Mermaid 1:30

I FINALLY KNOW WHAT I WANT TO BE WHEN I GROW UP!
WHAT?

AN ANIMATOR!
...A MERMAID!

...AND THE PART WHERE THE SEA WITCH TURNS INTO THAT GIRL, IN DISGUISE?! OH MY GOSH! I KNOW! SO GOOD!!

YOU GUYS TALKIN' ABOUT "THE LITTLE MERMAID"?

YEAH.
WHY, HAVE YOU SEEN IT?

YUP. IT WAS REALLY GOOD.

Before my two front teeth could be taken OUT, my braces had to be taken OFF.

THERE YOU GO!
...FEELS SO WEIRD AND SMOOTH!

WHEN MOST PEOPLE GET THEIR BRACES OFF, IT'S BECAUSE THEIR TEETH ARE FINALLY PERFECT!

BUT NOT YOU!

The last day of school came and went.

HAVE A FUN CHRISTMAS!

THANKS... HAVE A NICE HANUKKAH.

Usually, the start of Winter Break is one of the most exciting times of the year.

But that year, everything served as a reminder of what was about to happen to me.

Season's Greetings
from
The Telgemeiers
Sue Denis
Will
Amara
Raina

Finally, right before Christmas, the dreaded day arrived.
OKAY, RAINA. JUST TRY AND RELAX.

IT'S GOING TO BE FINE.

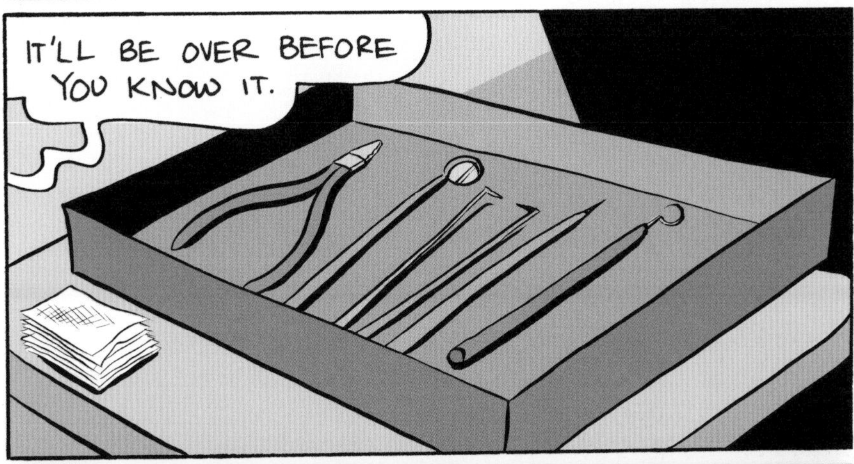
IT'LL BE OVER BEFORE YOU KNOW IT.

JUST TRY TO RELAX...

MOM! HEY, MOM!
BOUNCE HOUSE

LOOKIT, MOM!

I'M GONNA JUMP!

ARE YOU WATCHING, MOM?

I'M WATCHING, RAINA.
CE HOUSE

JUMP...

BOUNCE!!

HOOK!

!

MOMMMMMMM!!
BOUNCE HOUSE

MY TOOTH! IT CAME OUT! DID YOU SEE IT?! DO YOU KNOW WHERE IT WENT?

EVERYBODY START LOOKING FOR A MISSING TOOTH!

I DON'T SEE IT.
WHOEVER FINDS THE TOOTH GETS AN EXTRA FIVE MINUTES IN THE BOUNCE HOUSE!
NOPE, NOTHING HERE.

WE'VE LOOKED EVERYWHERE, HONEY. I THINK IT'S GONE.
BUT I NEED IT!!

YOU NEED IT?
HOW'S THE TOOTH FAIRY GONNA LEAVE ME MONEY IF I DON'T HAVE MY TOOTH?!!

I'M SURE THE TOOTH FAIRY WILL STILL VISIT YOU.

SHE'S MAGIC, SO SHE KNOWS YOU LOST YOUR TOOTH AT THE CARNIVAL.

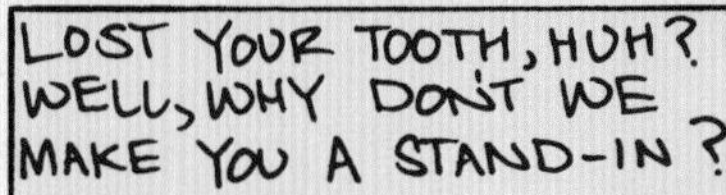
LOST YOUR TOOTH, HUH? WELL, WHY DON'T WE MAKE YOU A STAND-IN?

NOW WE'LL WRITE YOUR NAME ON IT, SO THE TOOTH FAIRY KNOWS IT'S YOURS.
?

...THERE.
YOU RUINED IT !!!
Raina

The next morning

MOM!! SHE CAME! THE TOOTH FAIRY CAME!!

"FOR RAINA, FROM THE TOOTH FAIRY"...

HOW COME HER HANDWRITING LOOKS JUST LIKE DAD'S?

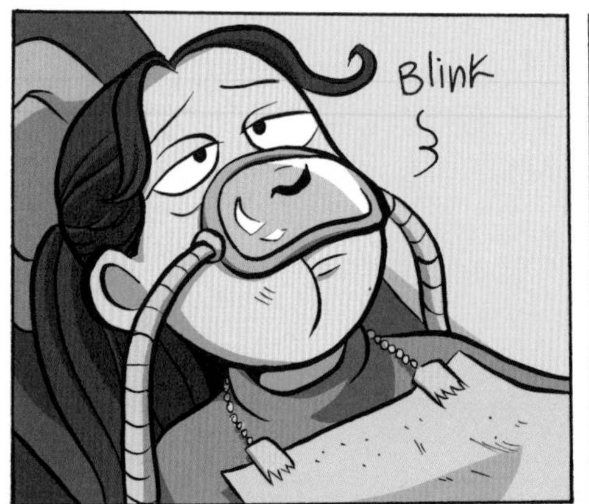
Blink

YOU'RE ALL DONE, RAINA. HOW DO YOU FEEL?
HHK.

JUST MAKE SURE SHE KEEPS THE GAUZE IN TONIGHT, OKAY? ONLY SOFT FOODS, TYLENOL, YOU KNOW THE DRILL.
THANKS, DR. GOLDEN.

I'LL SEE YOU IN A WEEK FOR THE FOLLOW-UP.
KKH.

DR. GOLDEN DDS
HAVE A MERRY CHRISTMAS!!

YOU WANT TO GO GET IN BED, HONEY?
Slump
NNNNNNGH...

ALL I WANT FOR CHRISTMAS IS MY TWO FRONT TEETH!

222

A few days later
YOUR NEW RETAINER IS HERE!

GET READY...

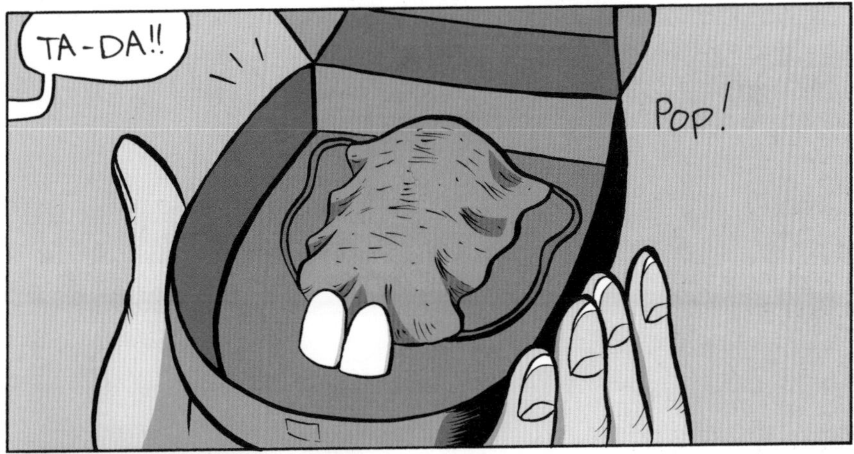
TA-DA!!
POP!

TRY IT ON!

SHE LOOKS PRETTY GOOD, HUH?
WOW!

YOU HAVE TO KEEP IT CLEAN, SO YOU SHOULD SOAK IT EVERY NIGHT WITH DENTURE CLEANER.

ONCE YOUR MOUTH GETS USED TO IT, WE'LL APPLY THE NEW BRACES.
Mouth of the month

THIS RETAINER MAKES ME LOOK SO NORMAL, MOM!!
VERY NORMAL.

SLIP
GRIND
CLICK
BUMP
GNASH

LET'S SEE YOUR NEW TEETH!
YEAH!

OKAY.

COOL!
CAN'T EVEN TELL THEY'RE FAKE!
WOW!
THEY LOOK GREAT!
NICE!

AAAAAAAAA!!!
flick

* FROM NEW KIDS ON THE BLOCK!

Aptos Middle School

CHAPTER FIVE

HIS NAME'S SEAN. HE TRANSFERRED HERE A COUPLE OF MONTHS AGO.

HE'S ON THE JUNIOR BASKETBALL TEAM, AND HE'S REALLY GOOD AT DRAWING.
123 ART

I'M PRETTY SURE HE DOESN'T HAVE A GIRLFRIEND... I'LL HAVE TO FIND OUT!!

HI.
OH! UH... HEH HEH... HI!

YIKES! THAT WAS EMBARRASSING... MY FACE TURNED TOTALLY RED.

I HOPE HE NOTICED!
HEY, RAINA!
TRAPPER KEEPER

OH! UH, HEY, SAMMY.
HOW'S IT GOING? HEADING TO MATH CLASS?

OH. UM, YEAH.
SEE YOU IN BAND LATER, OKAY?
SURE.

HOW'S YOUR TINY-TOT SIXTH-GRADER BOYFRIEND?

HE'S NOT MY BOY-FRIEND, MELISSA.
WHOA, WHAT HAPPENED?

I DUNNO, I... I THINK I MIGHT LIKE SOMEONE ELSE.
WHO?

SEAN.
THE ONE ON THE BASKET-BALL TEAM?

YEAH!
HE'S CUTE! HEY, VALENTINE'S DAY IS COMING UP! YOU SHOULD ASK HIM OUT!

WHAT?! ME?!
SURE! ASK HIM TO THE DANCE OR SOMETHING!

I COULD NEVER DO THAT!
WHY NOT?

I'D WANT HIM TO ASK ME.
AHHHHH...

A full week later...
SO-O-O-O-O-O-O!!... ARE YOU GUYS GOIN' TO THE VALENTINE'S DANCE?

SAY "YES," SAY "YES," SAY "YES," SAY "YES"...
I DUNNO.

DARN!!

HEY, RAINA! ARE YOU GOING TO THE VALENTINE'S DANCE?

I DUNNO.

WHAT'S WRONG?

FOOD STUCK. UNDER MY RETAINER... NNNNGH... IT FEELS SO WEIRD. UGH!

SO JUST TAKE OUT YOUR RETAINER.
I CAN'T! MY TEETH ARE ATTACHED TO IT.

I'M NOT GOING TO TAKE MY TEETH OUT IN FRONT OF EVERYONE!

POP!

GSHHHHHHHHHHHHHHH

SLRRRRRP

PTOO

MUCH BETTER.
CLNKL!

I FOUND OUT FROM STEVE: SEAN'S DEFINITELY NOT GOING TO THE DANCE TOMORROW.
AW, MAN!!

BUT YOU SHOULD STILL GO! IT'LL BE FUN. ME AND KELLI AND KARIN AND EMILY AND NICOLE WILL ALL BE THERE... KAYLAH AND JUAN ARE GOING...
WELL... MAYBE I'LL GO.

The next day
SO... YOU'LL BE AT THE DANCE LATER, RIGHT?
YEAH... I GUESS SO, SAMMY.

GOOD— I HAVE SOMETHING TO GIVE YOU.

SEE YOU THERE!

I FEEL SICK.

Later
BOOM BOOM

WHY DO I FEEL LIKE I WANT TO BARF?

BOOOMMBA BOOM
CAFETERIA
EXIT
VALENTINE'S DANCE
4-6 PM

BOMBA BOOM BOOM BOOM PBUM BUM BOOM
EXIT
VALENTINE'S DANCE
4-6 PM

BOOMBOOOMBOOMBOOMBABOOM
CAFETER
EXIT
VALENTINE'S DANCE
4-6PM

HI, MOM.
HONEY! YOU'RE HOME EARLY.

YEAH. I WASN'T FEELING GOOD, SO I DIDN'T GO TO THE DANCE.
AW. WELL, SIT DOWN AND TAKE IT EASY, KIDDO.

BUT SUDDENLY, I FEEL A LITTLE BIT BETTER!

SO THE DANCE WAS PRETTY FUN! YOU SHOULD'VE BEEN THERE.
EHHHH... IT'S OKAY.
shrug

YOUR LITTLE BOYFRIEND WAS STANDING AROUND BY HIM-SELF THE WHOLE TIME, THOUGH.
AAAAA! ARE YOU SERIOUS?! I TOLD HIM I WAS GONNA BE THERE.

HE'S PROBABLY SUPER MAD AT ME...I HOPE HE'S NOT MAD.

BAND!

HEY.

HEY... WHERE WERE YOU YESTERDAY?
UH... I WASN'T FEELING GOOD, SO I WENT HOME.

OH.

WELL, ANYWAY, HERE. THIS IS FOR YOU.

...I'LL OPEN IT LATER.
SHOVE

LOOK... JUST FORGET IT, OKAY?

JUST FORGET IT.

Later
WELL... GUESS I'LL SEE WHAT'S IN THE BAG...
WALGREENS DRUG

To: Raina
From: Sammy
Happy Valentine's Day!

Chocolate
WALGREEN DRUG

...PRICE TAG!
Chocolate
2.99

Sammy never spoke to me again after that.

Which I guess I deserved.

But I had other things to think about...

And, still others!

A BRACE-FACE! I'M GONNA BE A BRACE-FACE AGAIN IN A COUPLE OF WEEKS.

WHICH MEANS I'M GOING TO GO BACK TO LOOKING LIKE A NERD AGAIN.

IT'S SO UNFAIR. I FINALLY GET THIS RETAINER, I FINALLY GET TO LOOK COOL FOR A LITTLE WHILE...

AND NOW I HAVE TO START BACK AT SQUARE ONE!

ACTUALLY, YOU'VE ALWAYS LOOKED LIKE A NERD.
YEAH, "COOL" JUST ISN'T THE WORD TO DE-SCRIBE YOU.

YOU GUYS ARE COLD. HOW COME YOU'RE ALWAYS SAYING THINGS LIKE THAT?
HEY, YOU WALKED RIGHT INTO THAT ONE.

YOU'RE THE ONE WHO CALLED YOURSELF A NERD, NOT ME.
WHO'S A NERD, NOW?

... NOBODY.
OH, SO YOU'RE A NOBODY!!
WHAT ELSE IS NEW?!

...WHAT'S HER PROBLEM?
OH, SHE'S JUST BEING A BABY.

And so:
poke
GRIND
POKE
push
TWANG
poke

TWISTTT
snap
TIGHTEN
PUSH

HERE SHE IS!

LET'S SEE, HONEY.

IT HURTS TO SMILE.

HI, RAINA... WHAT ARE YOU DOING?

MASHING MY FACE INTO THE COUCH CUSHIONS.

IT'S THE ONLY THING THAT MAKES MY TEETH FEEL BETTER.
DINNER-TIME...

BUT YOU KNOCKED THEM CLEAN OUT A YEAR AGO... AND HAD THEM REMOVED AGAIN AT CHRISTMAS. HOW COULD BRACES BE SO MUCH WORSE?
Jell-O

ALL OF THAT WAS NOTHING COMPARED TO THE PAIN I AM FEELING RIGHT NOW.

The next day
OW... I NEED TO GET MY MIND OFF MY STUPID TEETH!

AH!

BANG

THE ATTACK ON PEARL HARBOR PROMPTED AMERICAN FORCES TO TRY AND... BLAH BLAH BLAH...

!!!

Braces DO stop hurting after several days.
I CAN SORT OF CHEW BREAD AGAIN!

But then...
YOU'VE GOT AN APPOINTMENT WITH DR. DRAGONI ON THURSDAY AFTER-NOON, HONEY.
AWW...

Every couple of weeks, you go and get them tightened.
380
101
SF Intl Airport
EXIT 1 MILE
I'M STARTING TO REALLY HATE THIS FREEWAY EXIT.

And then you start all over.
OPEN...

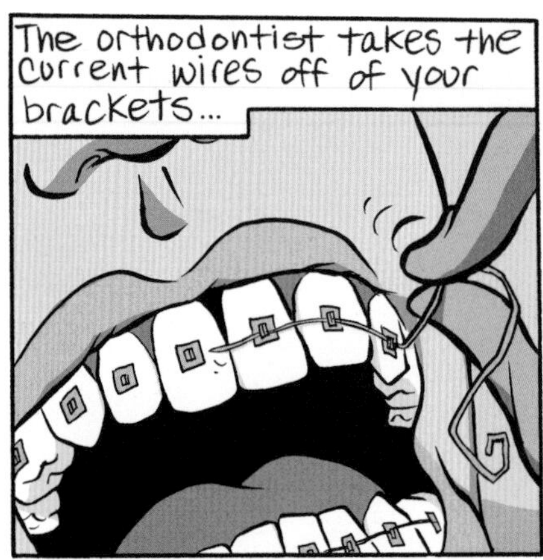
The orthodontist takes the current wires off of your brackets...

...and puts new wires on.
wiggle
twang

And then he TIGHTENS THEM.
TWIST! TWIST!
TWIST!

The ends of the wires are clipped off...
Snip!

...AND WE'LL SEE YOU AGAIN IN TWO WEEKS!

Before I Knew it, my birthday rolled around again.

OKAY. YOU ARE THIRTEEN YEARS OLD.
I KNOW. IT'S CRAZY!

IT'S TIME YOU KISSED YOUR FIRST BOY, I'D SAY.
HUH?!

COME ON, RAINA. EVERYONE KNOWS YOU HAVE THE HOTS FOR SEAN...
EXCEPT FOR SEAN HIMSELF!

IT'S TIME TO MAKE A MOVE. IT'S TIME TO MAKE AN IMPRESSION.

IT'S TIME FOR A MAKEOVER!!
AAACK! HANG ON! WAIT!!
CABOODLE
GRAB

DO YOU KNOW HOW TO SHAVE YOUR LEGS?
UM, YES.
GOOD. HOW SHORT IS YOUR SHORTEST SKIRT?

AND YOU HAVE GOT TO START USING SOME HAIR SPRAY ON THESE "BANGS" OF YOURS.
NICOLE, WHAT IS THE POINT OF ALL THIS?

SEAN'S ONLY GONNA GO FOR YOU IF YOU GLAM IT UP A BIT.

HOW THE HECK DO YOU KNOW THAT?!
HE TOLD ME SO.

SEAN TOLD YOU?. DOES THAT MEAN YOU TALKED TO HIM ABOUT WHAT HE LIKES IN A GIRL?. DOES THAT MEAN...

...YOU TALKED TO HIM ABOUT ME?!

YUP.

WOW. UM. I GUESS IF HE REALLY SAID THAT'S WHAT HE LIKES...

HE ALSO SAID HE LIKES TUBE TOPS.
AND FISHNET STOCKINGS.
AND BANGLE BRACELETS. LOTS OF 'EM.
AND NOSE PIERCINGS.
AND HIGH-HEELED BOOTS!

And so:
THERE! SEAN'S GOING TO LOVE IT !!

KKTHPLBBT!!!

HA HA HA
HA HA HA HA
HA Hee HA
HA
HA
WAAAAIT A MINUTE...
HA HA
HA HA HA
HA HA HA HA
HA HA
HA
HA
Hoo HA
HA
Hee

SEAN NEVER ACTUALLY TOLD YOU ANY OF THAT STUFF, DID HE.
NOPE.

WE WERE JUST MESSING WITH YOU.
YOU HAVE TO ADMIT, IT WAS KINDA FUNNY.

BUT WHAT IF I'D BELIEVED YOU GUYS?? WHAT IF I'D REALLY GONE TO SCHOOL ALL MADE UP?
THAT WOULDN'T HAVE BEEN VERY FUNNY.

IT WOULD'VE BEEN HILARIOUS!!

YOU TAKE EVERYTHING WAY TOO SERIOUSLY, RAINA.

YOU'VE GOT TO LOOSEN UP A LITTLE! LEARN TO LAUGH!

DON'T BE SO UPTIGHT!!
SHOVE!

Later
Tighten
Tighten
Tighten
EASY FOR HER TO SAY!!

WHAT IF IT WAS TRUE? WHAT IF SEAN REALLY WOULD NOTICE ME IF I DRESSED DIFFERENTLY?

WOULD I BE WILLING TO CHANGE, JUST FOR HIM?

220
222

SO FAR, BEING A TEENAGER IS NO FUN AT ALL.

calvin and Hobbes

CHAPTER SIX

The summer between seventh and eighth grade was mostly uneventful.

The weather was cold (like always), so I stayed inside a lot...
FLOUNDER, DON'T BE SUCH A GUPPY!

pretended I'd given Sean my phone number...
"HELLO? YES, THIS IS RAINA...SEAN?!"
1:24

mooned over a certain someone's picture...

and avoided the obvious.
HONEY, IT REALLY IS TIME YOU STARTED WEARING SOME SORT OF BRA...
MOMMMMMM!!!

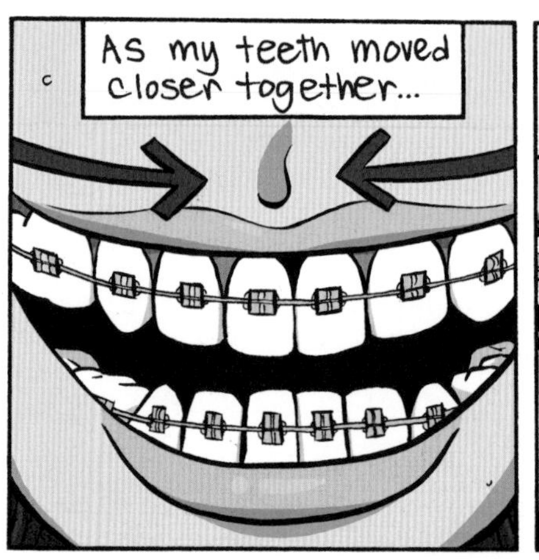
As my teeth moved closer together...

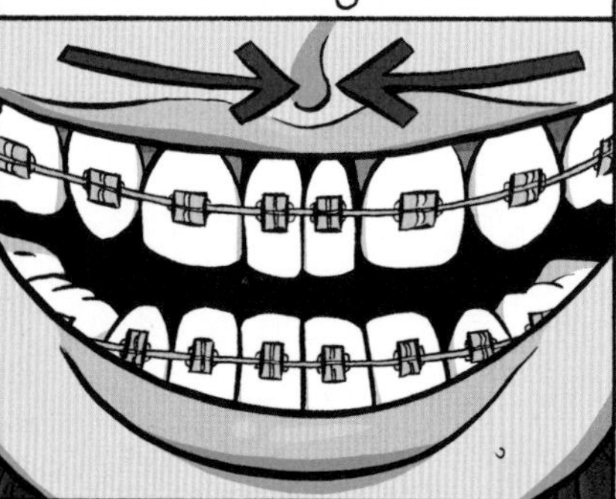
The fake teeth in the empty space were shaved down little by little.

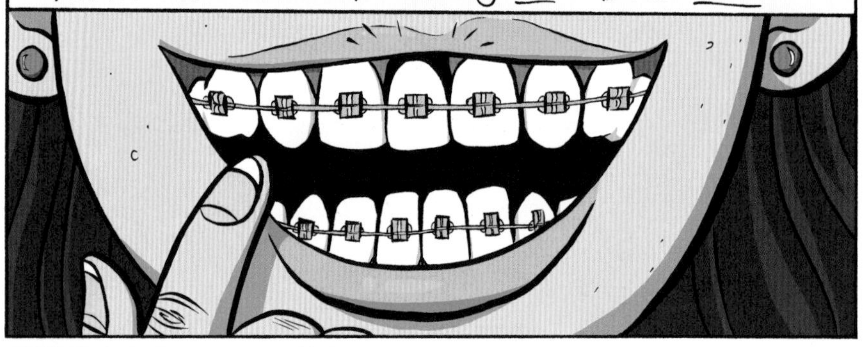
By the time eighth grade started, the two fake teeth had been replaced by one fake tooth.

I just hoped no one could tell.
GIRL, YOU NEED TO START USING A BETTER HAIR CONDITIONER.
MY BROTHER HAS THAT SHIRT... IT'S KIND OF A BOY'S SHIRT.
ESPRIT

Eighth grade was weird. We were all going through puberty, and at different rates.
Hair suddenly curly
Taller, hips wider
Chest got huge
Acne
Gloomy

Everyone was very preoccupied.
HAIR
CLOTHES
PIMPLES
MAKEUP
DIETING
ETC.
WHATEVER HAPPENED TO TALKING ABOUT CARTOONS?

But, the boys seemed to notice, and acted accordingly.
W-PWING!!!

The only boy who didn't seem to notice what was going on, was... well... guess.

SEAN'S NEVER GOING TO PAY ATTENTION TO YOU.
HE'S TOO MUCH OF A BASKETBALL-BRAIN.

IF IT DOESN'T HAVE TO DO WITH THREE-POINTERS OR MICHAEL JORDAN, HE ISN'T INTERESTED.

Girls' Basketball Team
TRYOUTS TODAY

YOU WANT TO TRY OUT FOR THE TEAM? SURE. DROP AND GIVE ME 25 PUSH-UPS.

...12...13...14...

PTOOM
PTOOM
PTOOM

WANG!

WHHHSSHHHH

I THINK I'M DOING... GASP, PANT... PRETTY GOOD!

BOYS' LOCKER ROOM
APTOS TIGERS
GO!!
GIRLS' LOCKER R

WOW, THAT WAS REALLY HARD. I'M BEAT.

BOYS' LOCKER ROOM

H'LO.

SLAM DUNK!!
BOYS

Girls' Basketball Team
1990-1991

1. Charmaign Lopez
2. Kiki Green
3. Shauna Chang
4. Elizabeth Wong
5. Rita Begonia
6. Esther Mendoza
7. Cherise Campbell
8. Tania Benz-Ortiz
9. Shantale Marie Evans
10. Yasmin Gutierrez
11. Silvia Armando
12. Letty Peng

Alternates: Sharita Johnson, Ellen Grace, Louisa Lee, Ai Suzuki, Candace O'Brien

SO HOW WAS SCHOOL, RAINA?

IT WAS OKAY... I TRIED OUT FOR THE BASKETBALL TEAM, BUT... I DIDN'T MAKE IT.

BASKETBALL! WHY, THAT'S... SINCE WHEN HAVE YOU BEEN INTERESTED IN SPORTS? IT MIGHT BE A GOOD THING YOU DIDN'T MAKE THE TEAM.

BASKETBALL MIGHT HAVE BEEN TOO DANGEROUS!
WHY?

YOU COULD'VE KNOCKED YOUR TEETH OUT ALL OVER AGAIN!

So you didn't make the basketball team. Big deal! Are you even that into sports anyway?
I guess not. But I've got to do something to get Sean to notice me!

You should draw him a picture! You're good at art.

What? No way! What would I draw? What would he do with it? What if I...
TELGE-MEIER?

I'LL TAKE THAT.

MR. FISCHETTI, IT'S NOT WHAT IT LOOKS LIKE! PLEASE, DON'T--

BLAH BLAH BLAH, BASKETBALL... BLAH BLAH BLAH, DRAWING... BLAH BLAH BLAH, SEAN...

WHO'S SEAN?!
AHHHHHHHH!!!
BODY GLOVE

Ha Ha
Ha
Ha
Ha
Ha
Ha
WELL...YOU WANTED TO GET NOTICED, RIGHT?

...IN THE FUTURE, MISS TELGEMEIER, PLEASE DON'T PASS NOTES DURING MY CLASS. THAT GOES FOR YOU, TOO, MELISSA.

I CAN'T BELIEVE THAT JUST HAPPENED! I WAS SOOOO EMBARRASSED!!
crunch!
HEY... AT LEAST SEAN ISN'T IN MR. F.'S CLASS WITH US.

BUT NOW EVERYONE KNOWS I LIKE HIM! WHAT IF THEY'RE ALL TELLING HIM RIGHT NOW?

UHHH... WHAT IF NOBODY CARES?

WELL THAT WOULD REALLY SUCK.

My crush on Sean was old news to everyone else, but it still consumed my thoughts a lot of the time.
15... 36... SEAN...

However, something interesting was starting to happen.
HEY, RAINA!

HEY, KAYLAH. HEY, EDWARD.
YOU GOIN' TO LUNCH?
YEARBOOK ORDERS
YEAH, WAIT UP.

Some of my friends had kinda-sorta-maybe boyfriends.

Boys who would hang around with us during lunchtime...

... and who would invite their other friends along.

Not all of them were cute, and not all of them were very mature...
WAIT, WHAT'S THIS? NEXT TO MY PEANUT BUTTER SANDWICH?

YAAAAARRGH! SPIDER!!
AIIEEE!!
rubber

But they were good for practice-flirting!
SHOVE!

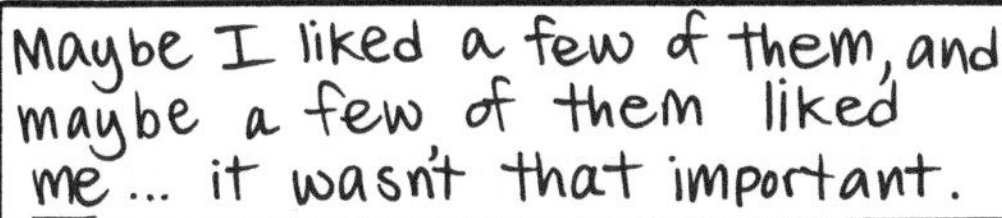
Maybe I liked a few of them, and maybe a few of them liked me... it wasn't that important.

PSST... WHAT'S THE ANSWER TO #6?
I'M NOT TELLIN' YOU!!

None of them were Sean.

But, boys were good for video game tips.
NINTENDO POWER

Boys didn't give me any flack about my appearance.
EVER THINK ABOUT TOOTH-WHITENING, RAINA? IT MIGHT BE A GOOD IDEA. FOR YOU.

And, they were willing to talk about important issues.
SO... ARE YOU GUYS READY FOR HIGH SCHOOL?!

HIGH SCHOOL! MAN, IT'S HARD TO BELIEVE WE'RE GRADUATING FROM EIGHTH GRADE IN ONE MONTH...
I KNOW...

LADIES AND GENTLEMEN, I HOPE YOU'LL ALL JOIN ME AT MY HOUSE NEXT WEEKEND FOR THE END-OF-SCHOOL PARTY TO END ALL PARTIES.
COOL!
THANKS, JUAN!

Parties presented a slight problem now that I was friends with boys.
HEY, EVERYONE! WHO WANTS TO PLAY SPIN THE BOTTLE?!

GULP!

BLAURGHL! GROSS! EWW!

PTEW!

PTEW!

YOUR TURN, JENNY!
HEE HEE!

...YOU HAVE TO KISS ANDREW!!
HA HA HA!!
EWW, GROSS!
HEY!

C'MON, RAINA, IT'S YOUR TURN! SPIN THE BOTTLE!

...I THINK I'LL PASS.
HUH??

I DON'T GET IT... HOW COME YOU WOULDN'T SPIN THE BOTTLE EARLIER?

YOU SAW HOW EVERYONE WAS ACTING. ANYBODY WHO HAD TO KISS SCREAMED "EW" AND "GROSS" AFTER.
crunch

I DON'T NEED SOME BOY TO YELL ABOUT HOW DISGUSTED HE WAS TO HAVE TO KISS ME.

BESIDES...

WHY WOULD I WANT MY FIRST KISS TO BE WITH ANY OF THESE GUYS?! THEY'RE ALL SO GROSS!
GRATS
ADUATES!

THE TRUTH IS... I WANT MY FIRST KISS TO BE PERFECT.

THE PERFECT GUY, THE PERFECT SETTING, THE PERFECT SONG PLAYING...

BUT WHEN I IMAGINE ALL OF THOSE THINGS, I IMAGINE MYSELF AS BEING PERFECT, TOO.
Hair
Skin
Body
Teeth

AND I DON'T THINK THAT'S GOING TO HAPPEN ANYTIME SOON!

Epilady
Revolutionary
NEW improved formula
OX
BALANCE
Sensitive Skin
BABY POWDER SOFT
TEEN
Spirit
NTI- PERSPIRANT
ex'cla-ma'tion
Cologne spray
gne en Vaporisateur
GREASELESS • MEDICATED
Noxema
SKIN CREAM
Cover Girl
NailSlicks

WELL! GOOD NEWS, RAINA.

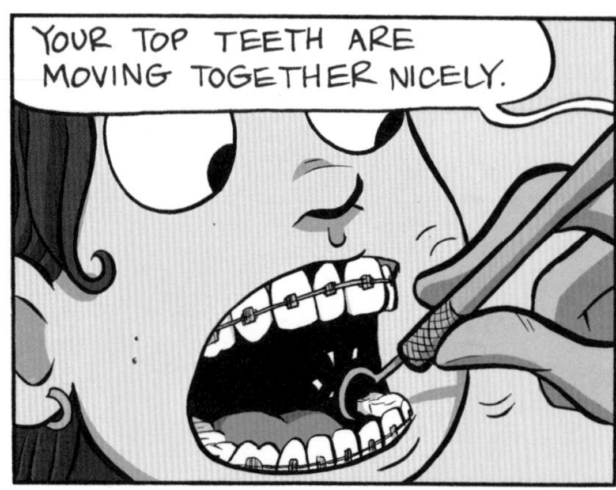
YOUR TOP TEETH ARE MOVING TOGETHER NICELY.

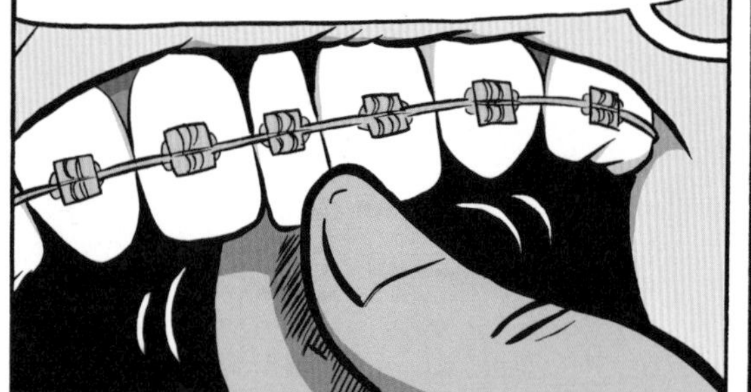
SOON, WE'LL BE ABLE TO REMOVE THIS LITTLE FAKE TOOTH IN THE CENTER, AND WE'LL PUT BONDINGS OVER YOUR NEW "FRONT" TEETH SO THEY LOOK NORMAL.

YOU DO HAVE A LOT OF GUM DAMAGE, THOUGH...

LET'S MAKE YOU AN APPOINTMENT WITH THE PERIODONTIST -- HE MIGHT BE ABLE TO HELP WITH THAT.

I DIDN'T EVEN KNOW THERE WERE THIS MANY KINDS OF "DONTISTS"...

At the periodontist's, a week later
YEP, YOUR GUMS ARE DAMAGED, ALL RIGHT!

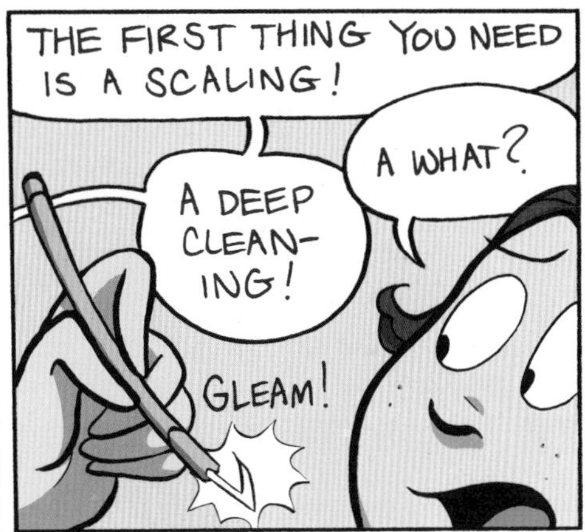
THE FIRST THING YOU NEED IS A SCALING!
A WHAT?
A DEEP CLEAN-ING!
GLEAM!

One shot of Novocaine and a couple of minutes later...
GRIND
SCRAPE
WHOA! BLOODY THERE! GAUZE, PLEASE! DON'T FIDGET, YOU'RE MAKING IT WORSE!!

...I was in some of the worst mouth pain of my life!
!!!!!!
OH, COULD WE GET HER A TYLENOL OR SOMETHING?

ROOM.....
SPINNING.....
C'MON, YOU'RE DONE.
Bruised!
Black & Blue!
Bloody!
FLOP!
BOOMP!

RAINA?...ARE YOU OKAY?
HONEY?
DID I PUKE?
NO...
HERE, DRINK SOME WATER...
WHAT JUST HAPPENED, DOCTOR?

WELL, WE DID A QUICK DEEP CLEANING OF THE GUMS, AND I GUESS WE DIDN'T WAIT LONG ENOUGH FOR THE NOVOCAINE TO WORK, AND WE COULD HAVE GIVEN HER LAUGHING GAS, BUT WE DIDN'T THINK SHE'D NEED--
WHAT?!!

MA'AM, PLEASE, THE OTHER PATIENTS WILL HEAR...
I DON'T CARE! MY DAUGHTER JUST FAINTED, THANKS TO YOUR NEGLIGENCE!!
BRITE

LET'S GO, RAINA... AND WE WON'T BE COMING BACK.

...THAT WAS PRETTY AWESOME, MOM.

T
B
G
P
Hi-C
ECTO COOLER
25¢ off
Expires Aug. 20
Aptos
Class of 1991
Commencement
Ceremony
June 12, 10:00 AM
Aptos Middle School Auditorium

...AND SO, AS YOU WALK OUT OF APTOS MIDDLE SCHOOL'S DOORS FOR THE FINAL TIME, REMEMBER THE THINGS YOU'VE LEARNED, THE PEOPLE YOU'VE BECOME, AND THE FRIENDS YOU'VE MADE ALONG THE WAY...

APTOS

SMILE, EVERYONE! SAY "CHEESE"!

WHAT ABOUT SOME PICTURES WITH SOME OF YOUR FRIENDS, HONEY?

NO, NO, THAT'S OKAY, DAD.

MY FRIENDS AREN'T A VERY SENTIMENTAL BUNCH.

That summer, I was a Girl Scout camp counselor for the last time.

The cutest boy I ever saw was sipping ciiiiiiiiiider through a straw!

And, I watched my "new" two front teeth appear!
I REMOVED THE LITTLE PLASTIC TOOTH FROM THE CENTER OF YOUR MOUTH...
...BECAUSE THE REST OF YOUR TEETH ARE SO CLOSE TOGETHER NOW!
COOL!
WE'LL BOND THE TWO "FRONT" ONES SO THEY LOOK NORMAL-SIZE, AND SHAPE THE ONES NEXT TO THEM A BIT.
...AND THAT'S GOING TO HURT, RIGHT?

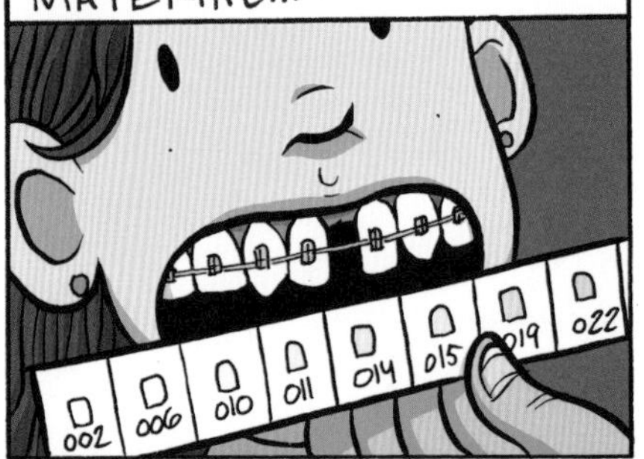
"ACTUALLY, IT'S NOT! THE DENTIST MATCHES THE COLOR OF YOUR TEETH TO THE BONDING MATERIAL..."
002
006
010
011
014
015
019
022

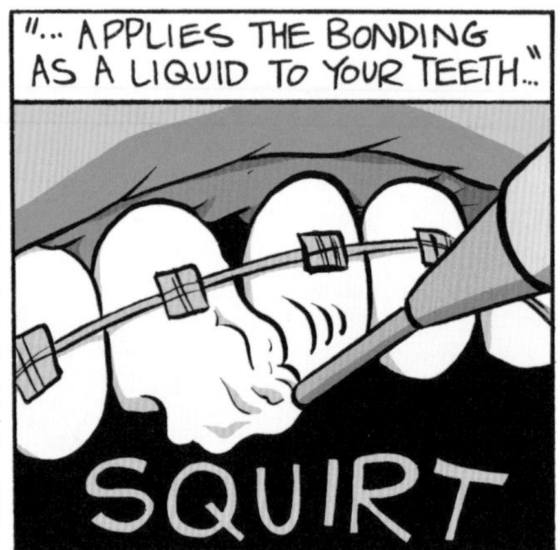
"... APPLIES THE BONDING AS A LIQUID TO YOUR TEETH..."
SQUIRT

"... THEN SETS THE LIQUID WITH A SPECIAL LIGHT."
BZZZZZZZZZZZZ

"THEN, HE USES A LITTLE BUZZING TOOL TO SHAPE AND SMOOTH THE BONDING."

WHAT DO YOU THINK? NOT BAD, HUH?

THEY ACTUALLY LOOK... KINDA OKAY.
GLAD YOU THINK SO!

BUT REMEMBER, JUST 'CAUSE THEY LOOK NORMAL, IT DOESN'T MEAN YOU'RE ALLOWED TO START EATING POPCORN AND JAWBREAKERS YET.
I KNOW, I KNOW.

Turquoise mock turtleneck!
Stylish fleece cardigan!

Socks that match turtleneck!
Cool black shoes with fat-laces!
Acid-washed denim!

Scrunchie!
Awesome earrings!
Almost-normal teeth!
Giant backpack!

HIGH SCHOOL, HERE I COME!!

OH! HI, MELISSA.
HEY.
STOP

IT'S TOO BAD WE'RE NOT GOING TO THE SAME HIGH SCHOOL.
YOU'LL BE OKAY.
6269

SO, YOU'RE NOT NERVOUS? NOT EVEN A LITTLE?
NOPE.

OH!! THIS IS MY STOP. SEE YA LATER!
LATER... HEY, RAINA?

DON'T FORGET TO SMILE!!
MUNI FAR

NERVOUS, NERVOUS,
NERVOUS, NERVOUS...

NERVOUS, NERVOUS,
NERVOUS, NERVOUS...

COOL!

MAN, THIS IS GREAT.

A WHOLE NEW SCHOOL, WITH NEW TEACHERS, NEW FRIENDS, NEW GUYS...

MAYBE THIS IS MY CHANCE TO START FRESH! A NEW, CONFIDENT ME! A NEW CHAPTER OF MY LIFE!

RAINA! OVER HERE!

HI, EMILY. HI, JENNY, ANDREW, KARIN, JUAN, KAYLAH, EDWARD, NICOLE, AND PERSON-I-DON'T-KNOW.
THAT'S MATT W.
HI.

HOW WAS YOUR SUUUMMER?♫
LOW-KEY.
REALLY?

MINE WAS A BLAST! JEN AND ANDREW AND I WENT ALL OVER THE CITY TOGETHER. IT WAS SO FUN!!
YEAH, REMEMBER FISHERMAN'S WHARF?
EEE! DON'T TALK ABOUT THAT!!
OH, AND THE TIME YOU GUYS ALL CAME OVER AND WE WATCHED "NIGHTMARE ON ELM STREET"?
HA HA HA!

Later
RAINA! HOW WAS THE FIRST DAY AT YOUR NEW SCHOOL?!
EXACTLY THE SAME.
DO WE HAVE ANY CHIPS?

ICH BIN FRAU CHAN. WIE HEIẞT DU? RAINA?
ICH HEIẞE "RAINA."
Ich heiße
Du heißt
SEHR GUT.

I'D LIKE EACH OF YOU TO WRITE A TEN-PAGE, DOUBLE-SPACED DISSERTATION OF "GREAT EXPECTATIONS" BY MONDAY...
THAT'S ONLY FOUR DAYS AWAY!!

...AND HERE'S ANOTHER TEXT FOR YOU TO READ, WHICH EXPLAINS IN DEPTH THE SOCIAL CONTEXT OF THE COLOMBIAN COFFEE TRADE IN THE NINETEEN-FORTIES...

IF THIS KEEPS UP, I'M GOING TO NEED A BRACE FOR MY BACK!!

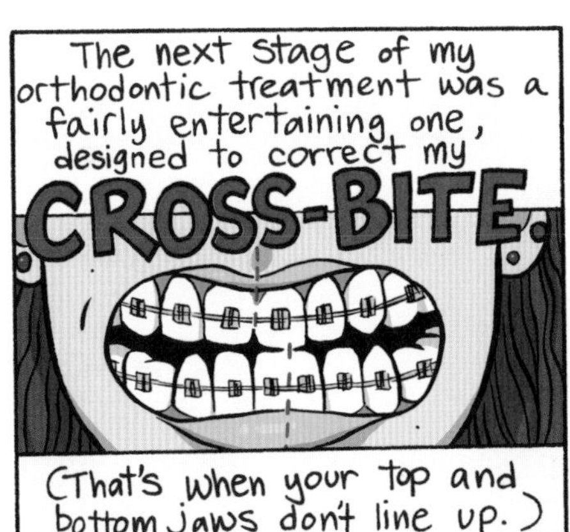
The next stage of my orthodontic treatment was a fairly entertaining one, designed to correct my
CROSS-BITE.
(That's when your top and bottom jaws don't line up.)

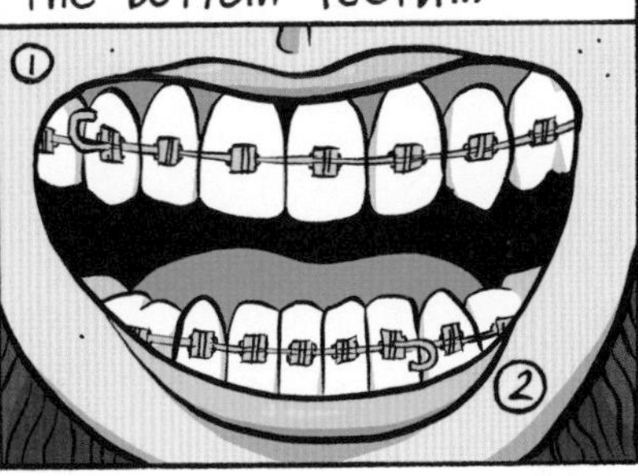
To fix this, little hooks are attached to specific brackets on the top and the bottom teeth...
1
2

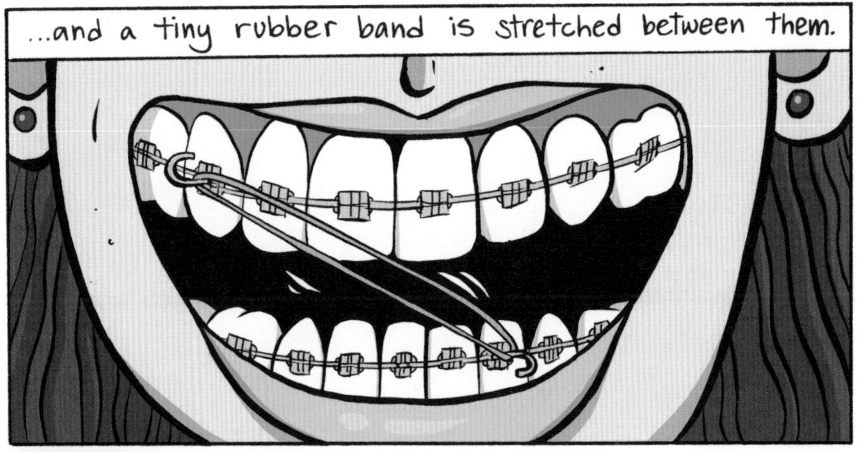
...and a tiny rubber band is stretched between them.

I CAN' OPEN MA MOUF ALL TH' WEY!
Twannngg!
YOU'LL GET USED TO IT!

So, tiny rubber bands joined the contents of my backpack.

0.3

Jones + Jones

Waxed Floss

Pick a Pick

E-Z Floss Threader

WAX

Fresh Mint

BRITE

ANTICAVITY TOOTHPASTE

Scape

Mouthwash

Along with travel toothbrush and paste, dental wax, floss, floss-threaders, a little box of toothpicks, and a tiny bottle of mouthwash.

COME ON, KARIN, THIS IS ALL STUFF FOR MY BRACES--
DOG BREATH! DOG BREATH!
Ha Ha!

AND I DON'T SUPPOSE THE REST OF YOU ARE GONNA STICK UP FOR ME, EITHER...
ERK!

EXCUSE ME. I'M GOING TO GO GET A SNACK.
...MILK BONE?

HA HA HA
HA HA HA
HA HA HA HA HA HA HA

HEY... I HAVE A FUNNY IDEA!

Beep
Beep
ONE... TWO...

THREE!
SHWWWP

HA HA
HA
HA
HA
HA
HA
HA
HA
HA
HA HA
YANK!

Snivel
Sniff
RAINA?

COME ON, WE KNOW YOU'RE IN THERE.
GO AWAY.
AW... YOU KNOW NICOLE AND KARIN WERE JUST PLAYING AROUND, RIGHT?
Roxy was Here

I DON'T CARE WHAT THEY WERE DOING-- THEY PULLED OFF MY SKIRT IN FRONT OF THE WHOLE SCHOOL!!
SLAM!
...AT LEAST YOU HAD LEGGINGS ON UNDERNEATH.

THAT'S NOT THE POINT. THEY HUMILIATED ME.
SPLASH!

BUT YOU HAVE TO ADMIT... IT WAS KINDA FUNNY...
WHAT?!

I CAN'T BELIEVE YOU GUYS. YOU EXPECT ME TO LAUGH OFF GETTING PANTSED IN THE COURTYARD?
NO, BUT--

FORGET IT. NONE OF YOU GUYS RESPECTS ME. I'VE HAD ENOU---

HEE HEE! UH, HI!
DON'T START CRYING... DON'T START CRYING...

...ARE THEY STILL WAITING FOR ME TO START CRYING?!

YOU GUYS WANT A REACTION FROM ME? FINE:

KARIN, I AM NOT A DOG.

NICOLE, I AM NOT A VAMPIRE.
OH, C'MON, I HAVEN'T CALLED YOU THAT SINCE--
NO.

AND I AM NOT GOING TO LET THE REST OF YOU DISRESPECT ME ANYMORE!

I'M DONE. GOOD-BYE.

RINNNG!!

NICOLE AND KARIN HAVE TEASED ME FOR YEARS... AND I ALWAYS LET THEM GET AWAY WITH IT.
DEUTSCHLAND

I GUESS DUMPING ON ME MADE THEM FEEL BETTER ABOUT THEMSELVES, IN SOME TWISTED WAY.

BUT, JUST BY STANDING UP TO THEM...
doodle
doodle

...IT'S LIKE I TOOK AWAY THEIR POWER!!
HA
HA
HA
doodle
doodle

After that, I essentially "broke up" with my old group of friends.

It was an amicable split— we still said hello in the halls, and acknowledged our shared pasts.

I was a little lonely now and then, but it didn't bother me.

I was happy to take life at my very own pace.

I'M THERESA!
I'M RAINA.
I KNOW!

WHAT?!
Lowell
YOU'RE THE ONE WHO MADE THE FLYER FOR THE FRESHMAN MEET -N- GREET, RIGHT? IT WAS SO WELL DRAWN!

WOW... THANKS!
SO WHAT MIDDLE SCHOOL DID YOU GO TO?
APTOS.
OH, THERE'S A GUY IN MY BIO CLASS WHO WENT THERE, MAYBE YOU KNOW HIM? HIS NAME'S SEAN.
SEAN?! HA HA! OH, YEAH. I DEFINITELY KNOW SEAN...

A little later
HEY, WHERE DO YOU NORMALLY EAT LUNCH? WANNA SIT WITH ME AND MY FRIENDS?
HEY, WHY NOT?

CHEETAZ

Dramatic
Mono-
logues

PRA
TEMPER
A PAINT
Mayor Jordan MUNI fare hike
25-cents-per-ride increase infuriates riders, residents
San Francisco

CHAPTER EIGHT

GETTING MY BRACES OFF! YESSS! I CAN'T WAIT!

IT'S HARD TO BELIEVE YOU'VE HAD THEM ON FOR THIS LONG!

BUT DO MY TEETH REALLY LOOK FIXED? THEY STILL SEEM A LITTLE FUNKY-LOOKING TO ME.

I'M SURE ONCE THE BRACES ARE ACTUALLY OFF, THEY'LL LOOK GREAT.

I'M SURE YOU'RE JUST SAYING THAT 'CAUSE YOU'RE MY MOTHER...

The big day finally arrived, a few weeks into my sophomore year.
♫ GETTIN' MY BRACES OFF...
MONTH OF THE MONTH

FIRST, WE'LL REMOVE ALL YOUR WIRES...
I'LL NEVER BE POKED AGAIN!

THEN WE PULL OFF ALL YOUR BRACKETS!
SCRRRRRRRKK!!

FINALLY, A QUICK POLISHING OF YOUR TEETH.
RRRRRRRR
RRRRRRR

READY TO SEE YOUR BRAND-NEW SMILE?...

YES, SIR, FOUR AND A HALF YEARS OF TREATMENT...

MOST OF WHICH WE PRETTY MUCH MADE UP AS WE WENT ALONG...

ALL TO GIVE YOU A NORMAL, HEALTHY-LOOKING MOUTH OF TEETH!
YAY!
WOW!
CLAP CLAP CLAP

...WHY DO THEY LOOK SO **WEIRD**?!

THEY DON'T LOOK THAT BAD! YOU'RE... JUST NOT USED TO THEM YET.

BUT THEY LOOK GREENISH! AND THEY'RE MISSHAPEN!
THAT STUPID RETAINER WITH THE PLASTIC TEETH ON IT WAS BETTER THAN THIS!!

WE'VE DONE THE BEST WE COULD... CONSIDERING WE BASICALLY REARRANGED YOUR WHOLE MOUTH...

ANYWAY, I HAVE SOMETHING THAT WILL CHEER YOU UP.

POPCOR

WHY THE LONG FACE, KIDDO?
MMM.
Celebratory Dinner

DR. DRAGONI TOLD YOU THEY CAN RE-BOND YOUR TEETH IN A FEW MONTHS.
MM-HMM.

YOUR TEETH SHOULD LOOK FINE AFTER THAT.

Food Drive
IF I COULD, I'D JUST HIDE MY FACE FOR THE NEXT FEW MONTHS!

RAINA! YOU JUST GOT YOUR BRACES OFF, RIGHT?
Econ Club
UMMM...

LET'S SEE!
LHS

LHS

NEAT.
LHS

DID YOU STUDY FOR OUR BIO TEST? I WAS UP HALF THE NIGHT READIN
WAIT, WAIT...

SO YOU GUYS DON'T NOTICE ANYTHING WEIRD? NOTHING ABOUT MY TEETH SEEMS BIZARRE TO YOU?
MMM...NOPE.
LHS

IS THIS SOME SORT OF TRICK? YOU LOOK CUTE!
YEAH, C'MON! WES AND BURT ARE WAITING FOR US AT THE FRONT GATE. WE'RE ALL GOING TO THE MALL FOR LUNCH!
CHESS CLUB
LHS
S.A.D.D.
Fridays 3pm
Rm. E106

WELL, THEN... WHAT ARE WE WAITING FOR?

ADMIT ONE
0009520

I didn't "get the guy," as they say. But Sean was always friendly to me.

Instead, I threw my passion into things I enjoyed, rather than feeling sorry for myself.

But the more I focused on my interests, the more it brought out things I liked about myself.
XMAS Lights
SKATE
SOPHOMORE HOP
October 7, 1992
7PM
Tickets
$5 w/ SAC
$7 w/o
$10 guests
Music by
Beyond Compare
CLASS OF 95
Poster Paint
And that affected the way other people saw me!

OPEN.
Dr. Golden reapplied the bondings to my teeth one final time.
BZZZZZZZZ
After that, I would have to start seeing my parents' dentist, Dr. Miller.
unclip
Dr. Golden only worked on kids' teeth, and he had kept me on as a patient much longer than normal.
TAKE CARE, OKAY?
...WANT TO CHOOSE A PRIZE FOR BEING SUCH A GOOD PATIENT?
HA HA... THAT'S ALL RIGHT.

OH, RAINA... IT'S THE END OF AN ERA!

NO TIME FOR SENTIMENT, MOM! I DON'T WANT TO BE LATE FOR THE SCHOOL DANCE !!

...AND CALL ME IF YOU NEED A RIDE HOME. HAVE FUN, HONEY!
THANKS, MOM! BYE!

EXIT

HOP
October 7, 1992
7PM
In the Court-yard
Tickets
$5 w/SAC
$7 w/o
$10 guests
Music by
Photos by

PHOTO
$15

PHOTOS
$15
1 large 8x10
10 small 3x5
20 wallet 2x3
+15
+20

ONE... TWO...
THREE...

The End!

Thanks to . . .

First and foremost, Dave Roman, who makes me smile every day.

Mom, Dad, Amara, Will, and Grandma, for being good sports and a great family.

Lea Ada Franco (Hernandez), Joey Manley, and everyone at Girlamatic.com, for giving a home to this project in its infancy. My friend and family dentist, Dr. Anne Spiegel, who evaluated the manuscript and gave me great encouragement along the way. David Saylor and Cassandra Pelham, for being a joy to work with. Phil Falco, John Green, and Stephanie Yue, for helping make my work beautiful. Judy Hansen, for being the best agent I could hope to have.

Alisa Harris, Braden Lamb, Carly Monardo, Craig Arndt, Dalton Webb, Hope Larson, Jordyn Bochon, Kean Soo, Matt Loux, Naseem Hrab, Rosemary Travale, Ryan Estrada, and Yuko Ota, for lending a helping hand during the final stages of production.

All of my friends who wrote me yearbook notes.

Everyone who has shared their own personal dental dramas with me.

The city of San Francisco, for giving me great backgrounds to draw!

Archwired.com, Janna Morishima, Heidi MacDonald, and Barbara Moon, for all their support and enthusiasm over the years.

Theresa Mendoza Pacheco, Marion Vitus, Steve Flack, Alison Wilgus, Zack Giallongo, Gina Gagliano, Bannister, Steve Hamaker, Seth Kushner, Neil Babra, and my extended family, wonderful friends, and readers, who have been invaluable.